D1516847

30

DAYS
TO A
MORE
RESILIENT
FAITH

Embracing the God of the Storm

30 DAYS TO A MORE RESILIENT FAITH

Barb Wooler *with* Wayne Hannah

BMH Books
P. O. Box 544
Winona Lake, Indiana 46590
bmhbooks.com

30 Days to a More Resilient Faith
Embracing the God of the Storm

Copyright © Barb Wooler and Wayne Hannah, 2016
ISBN: 978-088469-317-8
REL022000 RELIGION / Devotional
Published by BMH Books, Winona Lake, IN 46590
bmhbooks.com

All Scripture quotations, unless otherwise indicated, are taken from
the Holy Bible, New International Version®, NIV®. Copyright ©1973,
1978, 1984, 2011 by Biblica, Inc.™ Used by permission of Zondervan.
All rights reserved worldwide. *www.zondervan.com*
The "NIV" and "New International Version" are trademarks registered
in the United States Patent and Trademark Office by Biblica, Inc.™

INTRODUCTION

THE OLDEST BOOK OF THE BIBLE, JOB, DEALS WITH THE OLDEST question of man: why do seemingly bad things happen to good people? Or put another way, if God is good, why is there suffering?

A thousand generations have asked this question, and their sages have done their best to answer, to make sense of suffering, pain, and evil. Part I includes 30 short readings – one for each day of the month – drawn from two sources: the Bible and the wisdom of contemporary thinkers. In Part 2 consists of reflections on the role of pain and suffering in life as told by a man who has lived most of his life with a painful disease.

While there are many facets to this complex issue, the conclusion drawn from both the Bible and the sages is this: God is in the midst of crisis and suffering, drawing people to Himself and into His purposes.

CRISIS

*a difficult, often dangerous
situation or event*

SUFFERING

*the anguishing impact
of crisis on humans*

TABLE OF CONTENTS

PART 1: 30-DAY CHALLENGE

PART 2: DISCIPLED BY PAIN—ONE MAN'S STORY

> *"When times are good,*
> *be happy; but when times*
> *are bad, consider this:*
> *God has made the one*
> *as well as the other."*
>
> *Ecclesiastes 7:14*

PART I
30-Day Challenge

DAY 1
The Crucible of Crisis
Read Psalm 119:67; James 1:2-4

Who in their right minds would prefer hard times to easy? Ask 100 people which they prefer, and 100 would answer the same: give me the GOOD TIMES!

So how does one account for two very strange statements I heard recently? At a small group meeting a woman started her word of praise to God by saying, "I thank God for my stroke." Then in May, while in Nepal assisting earthquake victims, I heard a man say, "I thank God for the earthquake."

Crazy, right? But consider the fuller context of both.

In the case of the woman, she was thankful for her stroke because it brought her back to the Lord and also was healing her relationship with her estranged son. Though walking is now a bit of a challenge for her body, in a figurative sense, her spirit has a new spring in its step!

The man in Nepal is a pastor, and he has good reason to thank God for the April 25, 2016, 7.8-magnitude earthquake! Though his life became very difficult since that fateful day, he rejoices because the earthquake has brought his neighbors to their church in search of a safe place to sleep. The close contact between believers and unbelievers has resulted in quite a few of his formerly lost neighbors finding Christ!

It makes one wonder if, as Paul and Silas left Philippi, they, too, were thanking God for the earthquake, which resulted in their early release from jail, and more importantly, in the salvation of the jailer and his family!

Such stories are not all that unusual. Many know of people whose lives have been completely turned around by tragedy. I recently heard a story of someone whose difficult temperament was utterly transformed by a cancer diagnosis. Today, she is a joyful person who is grateful to God for all the friends she discovered she has. She never knew such joy B.C. (before cancer).

So, there's obviously another side to suffering, a side we could call an "inconvenient truth." This truth is hinted at by the Apostle James in his bizarre statement, "Consider it pure joy…whenever you face trials of many kinds" (James 1:2).

For these 30 days, we will consider the ubiquitous presence of "things-going-badly" in life. We may reach some surprising conclusions about crises, ourselves, the human experience, and yes, even about God.

DAY 2

God Uses Crisis to Move People – Geographically

Read Genesis 45:5, 46:1-4; Acts 8:1

MY THOUGHTS ON THE SUBJECT OF CRISIS HAVE EVOLVED A LOT FROM when I was first approached by Encompass World Partners about developing a Crisis Response ministry. To be honest, at that time I wasn't sure crisis ministry was a good match for me. But all that changed when I looked at the role of crisis in the Bible, and I came to a conclusion that left me wildly passionate about serving in crisis.

What conclusion did I reach? I saw that God uses crisis to move people, to change people's hearts, minds, and even their geography. The crucible of trial awakens; it shakes us from life's patterns and routines so that we are listening differently; it readies our mind to see afresh. But God uses crisis to move people geographically? Really? Yes, even geographically. Consider these well-known examples.

ISRAEL INTO EGYPT

When God wanted Israel to go into Egypt where they would grow into a great nation, how did He move them there? He sent a severe-famine (crisis) and as food grew scarce, the patriarch Jacob had no choice but to seek provisions in the only land that still had food: Egypt.

His sons were welcomed by the "Egyptian" official, and returned home with bulging grain sacks. Turns out that this generous official in Pharaoh's court was none other than Joseph, their brother!

So…how did brother Joseph end up in Egypt? It was by his brothers' wicked betrayal (crisis) years before, when they treacherously sold him to traveling merchants *happening by* on their way to Egypt.

Another geographic migration brought on by crisis was 430 years later, when God used ten horrific plagues (crises) to bring Israel, now a vast nation, out of Egypt.

MOBILIZING THE EARLY CHURCH

After Pentecost the church was exploding; Jerusalem was Christianity-Central. Believers were living and fellowshipping together, and their numbers grew daily as they anxiously awaited Jesus' return.

But weren't they forgetting something? Oh, yeah, the Great Commission. Their town, Jerusalem, was only Phase I! So how would God move the church into Judea, Samaria, and the ends of the earth? Through persecution (crisis) ignited by Stephen's martyrdom (crisis).

So we see throughout history that God uses crises – famine, betrayal, plagues, persecution – to move people into His good and perfect purposes.

DAY 3
God Uses Crisis to Move People – Changing Hearts
Read Acts 9:15-16, 14:22; 2 Corinthians 11:23-29

Saul of Tarsus. The best of the best. Sincere. Zealous. Smart. Highly educated. Passionate in his zeal for God. And dead wrong.

Suffering is central to Saul's story. It starts with his inflicting suffering on the church to destroy it, which ironically, God uses to spread the church. Then after two years, God's purposes in the persecution having been accomplished, the tables turn and now Saul is on the receiving end of the suffering. But let's go back to the beginning of the story.

GOD'S CHOSEN VESSEL TO SUFFER
On the road to Damascus, Saul is traveling with documents authorizing him to capture, imprison, and even kill followers of Jesus. Suddenly, a bright light flashes from heaven and strikes him down. A voice from heaven says, "Saul, Saul, why are you persecuting Me?" It is the voice of Jesus! (Jesus' words answer forever the question, "Where is Jesus in my pain?" – a subject for another day.)

Now blind, Saul's posse guides him to the home Jesus had indicated, and for three days he sits in darkness, in stunned silence and awe, wondering how he could have been so wrong! At the end of those three painful days, Saul emerges a man with a completely changed heart.

As it turns out, Saul – now going by his Greek name Paul – is God's chosen means to spread the church. Pre-conversion, this happened unintentionally, on his part anyway, as he scattered the church through persecution. But after his conversion the persecutor becomes the persecuted, and he suffers as few others in all of church history. All to take the gospel to the Gentiles.

God said of Saul, "[He] is my chosen instrument…I will show him how much he must suffer for my name." This prophecy proves true, and who can read without emotion Paul's long litany of suffering in 2 Corinthians 11:23-29?

It was not out of vindictiveness that God allowed Paul to suffer; it's just what was required in order for Paul's mission to be completed. One time when Paul had reached his limit, God lovingly appears to him in a dream to strengthen him. "Do not be afraid [Paul]," God says, "I am with you and no one is going to attack and harm you…" (Acts 18: 9-10).

Paul spoke from deep experience when he wrote, "We must go through many hardships to enter the kingdom of God" (Acts 14:22).

DAY 4:
God Uses Crisis to Move People – Changing Minds
Read Jonah 1, 3:1-3

No discussion of God's using crisis to move people is complete without dealing with the uncomfortable subject of how He uses crisis to change rebellious minds. Sadly, there are way too many Bible examples from which we can draw! Pharaoh. The Israelites in the desert. The Israelites in exile….

But the best example of God's using crisis to change someone's mind is this one.

GOD'S COMPASSION FOR MOSUL
God's heart was broken because of the wickedness of the people of Mosul (Iraq), the modern name for Nineveh. God called the prophet Jonah of Galilee to go preach to the Ninevites; perhaps they would repent and be spared God's judgment.

What a privilege to be chosen from among all people to be God's envoy! But we all know that's not how Jonah saw it. From Galilee, an obedient Jonah would go north and east to Nineveh, but instead our disobedient Jonah went south and west.

Oh, what misery he could have been spared if only…. But Jonah's mind was made up.

Running to Joppa, he boards a ship going anywhere but Nineveh. In exhaustion he falls asleep in the bottom of the vessel – running from God is hard work! We all know the story – big storm, thrown into the sea, God sends a big fish, Jonah swallowed alive….

How miserable it must have been in the belly of that fish! Stench. Half-eaten fish floating. Seaweed tangling. Ears paining in the deep. Fear… Think of it! It had to be terrifying!

Still, even in all that nastiness, it took three whole days of agony – of crisis – for Jonah to change his mind.

Finally, Jonah prayed: "When my life was ebbing away, I remembered you, Lord, and my prayer rose to you…I, with shouts of grateful praise, will sacrifice to you. What I have vowed I will make good." (Jonah 2:7, 9)

The fish vomited Jonah onto land, and the soggy, smelly prophet wobbled toward Nineveh, shakily at first, but strength grew with each step of obedience. The Ninevites repented and God "relented and did not bring on them the destruction he had threatened" (Jonah 3:10).

DAY 5
The WHYs and WHATs Behind Suffering
Read Romans 8:28; Job 1:6-8

THE WHYs IN LIFE ARE TRICKY, AND THIS IS NEVER TRUER THAN when it comes to WHY God allows a trial.

Maybe it's to move someone geographically – "Their house burned down because God wants them to move to Texas near their son."

Or is it to change someone's heart? – "God is teaching that person not to be arrogant."

Maybe it's to change someone's mind? – "He got fired so he'll stop refusing God's call to ministry."

When it comes to the WHYs behind trials and crises, filling in the ocean-wide gaps between our knowledge and God's is sketchy at best and dangerous at worst. Too often we get it all wrong, which only makes it harder for the person in crisis.

JUDGING

Of course, Exhibit A is the experience of Job. Job's comforters thought for sure they knew why he was suffering: it was because of secret sin in his life. But the truth was just the opposite, wasn't it? Indeed, Job was targeted for trouble precisely because he was upright, not because of sin in his life. God was confident Job's faith would withstand Satan's worst. So Job's comforters' speculation led them to a conclusion exactly opposite from the truth.

COLLATERAL EFFECTS

Sometimes a trial touches us while the real target is someone else. For example: An unsaved nurse needs to meet you, so you land in the hospital. Or your insurance man is struggling with suicidal thoughts and needs hope; of course the natural connection between you and your insurance man is a claim. Ouch!

If there's any truth to the theory of "Six Degrees of Separation" – the belief that every person on the planet is six or fewer people away from all others – it is quite possible that the primary reason trouble may come to me may at times be for someone else, someone I may not even know!

Though the WHYs of trouble are often too sketchy for conjecture, we can at least be confident about the most important thing: the WHAT of hardship – that God is wringing every ounce of good out of trials touching those who love Him.

DAY 6

All That We Don't know About Trouble

Read John 16:33; James 1:2, 12;
1 Peter 1:6-9, 4:12; Hebrews 12:5-13

When questioned about the existence of God, Albert Einstein is alleged to have answered: "Man knows perhaps three percent of all there is to know. That leaves 97 percent we do not know. Isn't there room in that 97 percent for God?"

In between the things we know are vast expanses of things we do not know. Navigating blindly through these voids most certainly leads to wrong conclusions, especially when those conclusions have to do with trouble in our lives.

Our loving Heavenly Father has not left us to navigate blindly through these oceans of unknowns. He has given us the necessary instrumentation – two essential guides – to lead us through space, time, and trouble so we can avoid being broken and shipwrecked on rocky cliffs of doubt.

GUIDE 1

The first divine guide is truth. While He hasn't revealed every truth that can be known, what truth He has revealed is a solid, trust-worthy guide through life's hazards.

Truths we know about trouble… It is:

- **EXPECTED** – Jesus guaranteed we'd have trouble (John 16:33), so why be surprised at our suffering "as though something strange were happening to [us]"? (1 Peter 4:12).

- **PURPOSEFUL** – Peter said trials purify and strengthen faith and result in heavenly reward (1 Peter 1:5-7).

- **REASSURING** – Trouble sent to correct us when we err proves we belong to Him (Hebrews 12:5-13).

- **GOOD** – Paul said God redeems good out of trouble (Romans 8:28).

GUIDE 2

The second divine guide is faith. Faith is the great bridger-of-gaps, the connector-of-dots that fills the spaces between the truths we know. Simply put, truth + faith = confidence during trouble.

DAY 7

The Uncomfortable Truth About Trouble:
God Could Stop It!

Read Ephesians 1:11

FOR THE NEXT TWO DAYS WE VENTURE OUT INTO WATERS THAT WILL feel choppy and uncomfortable regarding the connection between God and trouble.

One month after 9/11, Christian apologist John Piper wrote an article entitled, "Why I Do Not Say, 'God Did Not Cause the Calamity but He Can Use It for Good.'" In it, he establishes a difficult but biblically irrefutable truth: that God chose not to prevent 9/11. Indeed, on that day – and every other – God was working "all things after the counsel of his will" (Eph. 1:11). Below are excerpts from that article.

"Among the 'all things' under God's sovereignty are the:

- fall of sparrows (Matthew 10:29)
- rolling of dice (Proverbs 16:33)
- slaughter of his people (Psalm 44:11)
- decisions of kings (Proverbs 21:1)
- failing of sight (Exodus 4:11)
- sickness of children (2 Samuel 12:15)
- loss and gain of money (1 Samuel 2:7)
- suffering of saints (1 Peter 4:19)
- persecution of Christians (Hebrews 12:4-7)
- repentance of souls (2 Timothy 2:25)
- gift of faith (Philippians 1:29)
- pursuit of holiness (Philippians 3:12-13)

- giving of life and the taking in death (1 Samuel 2:6)
- crucifixion of his Son (Acts 4:27-28).

"From the smallest thing to the greatest thing, good and evil, happy and sad, pagan and Christian, pain and pleasure – God governs them all for His wise and just and good purposes (Isaiah 46:10).

"Lest we miss the point, the Bible speaks most clearly to this in the most painful situations. Amos asks, in time of disaster, 'If a calamity occurs in a city has not the LORD done it?' (Amos 3:6). After losing all ten of his children in the collapse of his son's house, Job says, 'The LORD gave and the LORD has taken away. Blessed be the name of the LORD' (Job 1:21). After being covered with boils he says, 'Shall we indeed accept good from God and not accept adversity?' (Job 2:10)

"IT IS A MYSTERY, INDEED, how God governs all events in the universe without sinning, without removing responsibility from man, and with compassionate outcomes!"*

* Piper, John, Desiring God, "Why I Do Not Say, 'God Did Not Cause the Calamity, but He Can Use It for Good,'" September 17, 2001, http://www.desiringgod.org/articles/why-i-do-not-say-god-did-not-cause-the-calamity-but-he-can-use-it-for-good, used with permission.

DAY 8

The Uncomfortable Truth about Trouble:
God is Complicit!

Read Genesis 37:26-28, 45:4-5;
Job 2:1-8; 2 Corinthians 12:7-10; 1 Corinthians 2:7-8

THIS IS OUR SECOND DAY OF VENTURING OUT INTO UNCOMFORTABLE waters concerning the connection between God and trouble. Yesterday we contemplated God's sovereign control over everything. Today's truth is perhaps even more uncomfortable! It is that (there's no escaping it). God is complicit in our trouble.

JOB
The best place to start is with the story of Job, the quintessential story of faith under fire. Was Satan free to strike Job at will? No, Satan had to ask permission from God, and God set boundaries on Satan's power to harm.

JOSEPH
It was Joseph's brothers who betrayed him. THEY sold him as a slave to merchants traveling to Egypt. But many years later, when his brothers came to the horrifying realization that Pharaoh's official was none other than their little brother Joseph, they heard Joseph's amazing statement: "And now, do not be distressed and do not be angry with yourselves for selling me here, because it was to save lives that God sent me ahead of you" (Genesis 45:5).

Years later he would reaffirm this conclusion to his brothers: "Don't be afraid…You intended to harm me, but God intended it for good to accomplish…the saving of many lives" (Genesis 50:19-20).

PAUL
God entrusted Paul with direct revelation and knowledge unlike any other man besides Jesus. So to keep him from becoming

proud, God gave him a "thorn in the flesh," also called in the same verse "a messenger of Satan" (2 Corinthians 12:7).

JESUS

And the most beautiful gift ever given, our salvation, which brings us richness and joy every day, is the result of the most horrific suffering and vile crime ever committed, when Satan struck Jesus on the cross (1 Corinthians 2:7-8).

While there are aspects of this mystery not to be grasped this side of heaven, what is abundantly clear is that the forces of heaven (good) and hell (evil) come together in pain. TROUBLE is where these opposite (but not equal) forces meet to work for entirely opposite ends: God to lift, bless, and strengthen; Satan to bring down, kill, and destroy.

Will our faith stand? Will trouble make us better or bitter? Which will it be?

DAY 9

The Strategic Place of Prayer in Crisis

Read Psalm 22:5-21; Matthew 26:39; James 5:13

WHATEVER YOU MAY THINK OF THE MOVIE *THE PASSION OF THE CHRIST* (Mel Gibson), I think the scene at the foot of the cross got a lot right. Looking down from the cross, Jesus sees a vile-looking "humanoid" (Satan) circling through the crowd. The creature's sneering grin grows deeper as each breath of the Savior becomes more labored. Satan's ancient plan will soon be realized.

Poetic license? Not so fast. But to find the source text one must leave the Gospels and go to the Psalms of David. Psalm 22, the prophetic account of the crucifixion, reads: "a band of evil men has encircled me….bulls surround me…roaring lions open their mouths wide against me…dogs have surrounded me…." Horrific. Evil.

The psalm continues, recounting the future prayers of the dying Lamb of God from the cross, "But you, O LORD, be not far off; O my Strength, come quickly to help me. Deliver my life from the sword…Rescue me from the mouth of the lions…."

Surely heaven and hell met at the cross! In a lesser, but very real way, the same is true during any crisis. Crisis brings people to their most vulnerable; and that's where heaven and hell rush in although for completely opposite purposes.

Our only weapon to wield, as demonstrated here by Jesus, is prayer, which penetrates the veil, touching the heart of the Father and breaking the resolve of the evil one. Prayer – simple, desperate, and earnest. Only prayer.

OTHERS WHO SOUGHT DELIVERANCE THROUGH PRAYER

PAUL
Three times Paul prayed for God to remove his thorn in the flesh. (2 Corinthians 12:7,8)

JOSEPH
The Bible records none of Joseph's prison prayers except those requesting wisdom to interpret dreams, but certainly this man of God prayed constantly to be delivered from prison.

JOB
Job sweetly yielded to God's will, offering up almost super-human prayers to Him who "gave, and . . . has taken away; may the name of the Lord be praised" (Job 1:21).

James agrees, writing simply, "Is anyone among you in trouble? Let them pray…" (James 5:13).

PRAYERS ANSWERED
All four would affirm that their prayers were answered, though the answers looked different from their requests:

- Jesus still was made sin, but rose in victory, opening the way between God and man.
- Paul was granted sufficient grace…but not healing.
- For years God answered Joseph's prayer for deliverance by granting him favor in the eyes of those in authority over him. Finally, at the perfect time, he was released from prison.
- Job was vindicated before his "comforters," but his losses were real.

DAY 10
A Crisis Prayer God Didn't Forget
Read Isaiah 49:15; Luke 12:6-7

GOD USED TWO THINGS TO MAKE ME PASSIONATE ABOUT A MINISTRY in crisis response. The first was studying crisis throughout the pages of Scripture, which has provided most of the source material for these devotionals. The second was an experience I had in the Philippines.

The story actually begins in Africa. In November 2013, I was in Bangui, Central African Republic, trying to recover from being sick. Too weak to do anything else, I listened to BBC radio. A special came on about Tacloban in the Philippines – a name that was new to me. Weeks before, the city had taken a direct hit from Super Typhoon Yolanda, and people were telling their stories, each one ending in tears. I was moved and remember praying something like, "Lord, please help these people! Bring eternal good out of the devastation! Use it to draw people to You."

Six weeks later I was back in the USA, working on helping war-torn CAR with food and seed. I confess my prayers for Tacloban were far from my mind…but not from God's.

Fast-forward exactly one year later. I had accepted the invitation of a missionary to see the results of his agency's response to a powerful typhoon that struck a year before in the Philippines. Landing in Cebu City heavily jetlagged, I flipped on the TV in my hotel room and found a one-year-anniversary documentary on "Super Typhoon Yolanda." It sounded very familiar. Then I remembered the BBC story I had heard on the radio a year before in Africa.

Traveling throughout Samar Island, we saw a land still heavily scored and pocked by the typhoon's strength. But the contrasting beauty of new life, new believers, and new church plants was stunning. I sat worshipping in a church plant, which hadn't existed a year before. As they sang, it all came back to me. I remembered my prayer from a year before, and realized I was sitting in the midst of God's answer! These were the people for whom I had prayed!

I had forgotten – but God had not. My prayer, slowly swallowed up by time and the demands of life, sprouted and grew in the soil of God's faithfulness. He joys in answering the prayers of His children.

DAY 11
The Blessing of ISIS
Read Psalm 94:16-19

AS OUR VAN BUMPED ALONG A WINDING ROAD THROUGH THE IRAQI countryside, my new Iraqi friend, Fada, and I conversed about many things. Finally I warmed to my favorite subject, "So, how did you come to know Jesus?"

Fada's story starts in Baghdad, where she was born and raised. Married now with two sons, she and her family were forced to flee Baghdad by Islamic militants called ISIS. With little more than the clothes on their backs, they landed in the Kurdish-controlled city of Erbil. Though they had been people of means before, paying for an apartment without income from a job quickly exhausted their resources. So it was that on the first day that they couldn't cover their rent, their landlord put them out immediately.

"I couldn't believe we were kicked out and living on the street!" Fada said. "I was so angry at God! Why would He allow us to be in such a shameful situation? But by the second day my anger was replaced with fear and desperation. We had already contacted every friend or family member we knew and had no one else to call.

"On the second day, a stranger approached us and asked why we were on the street. When we told him he said, 'Why stay on the streets? My church will help you.'

"So we followed this man we didn't know to his church. These strangers took us in and treated us more kindly than our own friends and family! Soon my boys and I started attending services, which is how I found Christ."

Though her story differed in detail, it contained a common thread I had been hearing in other faith stories from Iraqi and Syrian

Christians. The common thread is that it was through the dreadful situations caused by ISIS and Muslim-on-Muslim violence that they found eternal life in Christ. I had heard this so frequently that I had started to think of ISIS, as outrageous as it sounds, as a great "evangelist"!

Wanting to try out the term on Fada, I said, "So, maybe we could say that ISIS is a great–," and at this point, to my utter surprise, she completed my thought with, "–blessing."

Yes, her family's losses were deep and real, but she could honestly affirm that ISIS was a "blessing" because ISIS chased them straight to the church and the waiting arms of her Savior.

DAY 12

Groaning
Part 1: Groaning Spoken Here

Read Romans 8:22-26

"We know that the whole creation has been groaning as in the pains of childbirth right up to the present time. Not only so, but we ourselves...groan inwardly as we wait eagerly for our adoption to sonship, the redemption of our bodies...In the same way, the Spirit helps us in our weakness...[interceding] for us through wordless groans."

Why, in a world that has been groaning since being subjected to the curse, should we be surprised at the amount of groaning we earth-dwellers do?

Romans 8:22-26 describes some of the groaning going on, which extends beyond mankind to the planet, to the entire universe, and even to the Holy Spirit! The word groan in this passage (Greek "stenazo") carries the idea of sighing, mourning, or crying out (as in anguish). It is sound rising out of deepest human pathos, an emotion so powerful one abandons words while retaining "audibles" described as moans, sighs, and groans.

We groan in sickness and in dying. We groan in brokenness and in pain. We groan in longing and in loss. We groan because we're stuck in bodies that die a little more each day. Oh, yes, we groan, longing to finally be able to put on our perfect, eternal bodies.

That the Godhead groans is in itself staggering, putting an end to the lie from the adversary that God is disinterested and aloof. The other side of the God-that-groans "coin" – the Happy God of which author John Piper has written extensively – is somehow easier to grasp. Yet the Scriptures present both as equally true as they are mysterious.

Returning to the passage, there is a profound blessing found here that we mustn't pass over. When the Bible states that the Holy Spirit groans, it is not a groan on human terms, most often accompanied by the rolling of eyes, a "tsk, tsk," and a "What? Not again!"

No. The groaning of the Spirit comes out of a bottomless reservoir of compassion. This groaning transcends mere feeling and rises to the Father in the form of prayers; not just prayers, but perfect prayers, prayers personally crafted by the Holy Spirit to precisely match both our need and the Father's will.

Only in the matrix of divine love could groaning be transformed into blessing. Oh the deep, deep love of Jesus.

DAY 13

Groaning
Part 2: An Aria Breaks Forth

Read 2 Corinthians 4:16-18; Psalm 86:1-4; 88:1-2;

OUT OF DEEPEST SORROW CAN RISE A RICHNESS AND BEAUTY ONE would never think possible. Timothy Keller tells of a man, Greg, who in the midst of deep brokenness and traumatic loss likened his deep suffering to an operatic aria. Keller writes, "[Greg] observed how in the middle of many operas there was a crucial aria, a 'sad and moving solo' in which the main character turned sorrow into something beautiful. And Greg said, 'This is my moment to sing the aria. I don't want to, I don't want to have this chance, but it's here now, and what am I going to do about it? Am I going to rise to the occasion?'" (Keller, *Walking with God through Pain and Suffering*, pp 164-165)

This aria can be heard and maybe even enjoyed by others, but can be fully known, understood, and savored only by heaven.

We have no doubt sung our share of such arias and have heard others' as well. It's that person who cannot stem the flow of tears each week during church. That is an aria.

It's someone, like my mother in her later years, who cannot get through even the first phrase of a prayer without getting choked up. They are longing for something. That is an aria.

Jesus at the tomb of Lazarus looked out at those mourning their friend. Though He knew they would soon be elated, their profound sadness moved Him. Jesus wept. This was an aria.

Arias are sung from desperate places such as ash heaps, from the belly of a great fish, or from the end of oneself when asked for an excruciating third time, "Peter, do you love me?"

Often those emerging out of deepest sorrow of soul have expressed, with a tinge of sadness, how they already miss the special intimacy they knew with God when He carried them through the darkest times. Those are arias.

Like Greg said, no one wants to sing the aria. Sad arias can be sung only by sad people, and nobody wants to be sad, crushed, broken. But when it's our turn, the unscripted, unrehearsed song can rise, if we let it, on a cue all its own when it can no longer be held back.

Arias weave sadness into something tender and beautiful. When it is our turn, will we sing?

> *"Bad things happen in the freedom that comes with life."*
>
> *– Pastor Jim Bull,*
> *Palmcroft Church,*
> *Glendale, Arizona*

DAY 14

Cleaning House – Chaff, Dross, and Dust

Read Hebrews 10:36; James 1:2-4

> *"For you, God, tested us; you refined us like silver."*
> *Psalm 66:10*

A CHURCH IN AUCKLAND, NEW ZEALAND, PURCHASED AN OLD BUILDING. Once a jewelry factory, the building had sat empty for years, so the group got busy cleaning. By the end of the day they had a large pile of dust and dirt to discard when someone got the brilliant idea of putting it through a furnace. After all, the dust was collected from the floor of a jewelry factory. Amazingly, the furnace did indeed reveal precious materials, and they walked away with $8,500! The next day they returned with the filthy, matted carpet and this time walked away with $3,500. And why not the ceiling tiles, too? – $350.

This story illustrates a truth from the Scriptures. The Bible likens faith to gold, silver, and precious stones. Mined straight from the ground, these precious materials look like humble hunks of rock. It's the work of the fire to consume the common materials, leaving behind something beautiful and precious.

But fiery trials do more than purify; they firm up and consolidate. Those precious, tiny bits in the floor sweepings from the jewelry factory had value, but far more so when brought together. Our fiery trials give faith and virtue a chance to "work out" together, strengthening those "muscles" *if* we allow it.

An untried faith is weak, reactive, clumsy, and naive. Honed by the heat and pressures of real life troubles, faith can become strong, measured, agile, and confident. The world of sports provides excellent examples to illustrate.

In NFL football, most teams look like sure playoff contenders in July, as teams practice with their own teammates. The real test comes in September, when they don their pads and play for real against a team not afraid to hit and hit hard. It is here that a team's true depth is revealed.

As boxer Mike Tyson astutely noted, "Everyone has a plan until they get punched in the mouth."

No one enjoys getting punched in the mouth! No one longs for trials and testing to come, but as the Apostle Peter aptly noted, "These trials will show that your faith is genuine. It is being tested as fire tests and purifies gold" (1 Peter 1:7a NLT).

When our time of testing comes, will we rise to the level of patient endurance?

DAY 15

An Argument from Silence: The Un-Prayer

Read 1 Thessalonians 3:3-4; Acts 9:16

FROM THE FIRST, PAUL WAS DESTINED FOR SUFFERING; AND SUFFER he did. Everywhere he went, he and his message brewed up trouble. The most despicable troublemakers were the Thessalonians – not the common people, but the leaders. Paul's initial ministry there was going along just fine. It was only when amazing things started happening – when the power of the gospel was unleashed and people responded – that trouble started.

The Jews become jealous when they saw people accepting Paul's message, so they went to the market place, rounded up unsavory characters, and started a riot. Unable to locate Paul, they grabbed some innocents and had them arrested. That night, under the cloak of darkness, the brothers sent Paul on to the next town.

Fifty miles later, Paul was teaching in the next town, Berea, and God was once again blessing his message with great fruit.

Now things get even uglier.

Back in Thessalonica, the haters heard that Paul's message was having success in Berea. Once again they rounded up their rabble-rousers and sent them off to destroy Paul's work there, too! These jealous leaders were just like those Jesus warned, saying, "Woe to you...you hypocrites! You shut the door of the kingdom of heaven in people's faces. You yourselves do not enter, nor will you let those enter who are trying to" (Matthew 23:13-14). They were really bad guys. Wolves!

In perfect contrast to those bad Thessalonians were the good Thessalonians. This church was so obedient, the only exhortation Paul could conjure up was to tell them to just "keep doing what you are doing, and do it more and more." They were really good people.

Knowing there were ravenous wolves living among his precious Thessalonian "sheep," Paul's prayers were extra fervent. It's exactly here where the insight on prayer for suffering people is gained, not just in what Paul prayed for them, but especially in what he did NOT pray. He does not pray that they will be spared persecution, but that they would not be shaken by it. Finally, Timothy comes with a positive report after which Paul writes, "...we kept telling you that we would be persecuted... For now we really live, since you are standing firm in the Lord" (1 Thessalonians 3:4, 8).

Certainly it isn't wrong to pray that our loved ones be spared trouble. The point here is simply that this was not Paul's first reflex as he prayed for his friends in trying circumstances; and this silence says a lot.

DAY 16
Part 1: No Graven Image
Read Romans 3:3-4; Exodus 20:3-4

AUTHOR ELISABETH ELLIOT HAD BOTH THE CREDIBILITY AND THE agility of mind and pen to speak concerning suffering. Her first husband was savagely martyred, her second died from cancer, and her third cared for her through a long, debilitating illness, which took her in 2015.

Evidence of the hard storyline Elliot's life took is that a novel she published, which closely mirrored her own story, was met with criticism by the Christian public at the time. The primary complaint about the book entitled, *No Graven Image*, was that it wasn't believable; certainly God would never subject one of His choice servants to such adversity!

Obviously those who complained: 1) were not familiar with Elliot's own story; and 2) didn't enjoy having their own "graven images" of what God is really like challenged. Elliot welcomed the criticism, which only confirmed the book's premise: that God is who He is, does as He wills, and answers to no one but Himself; any other god we erect in our hearts is a graven image.

How do our own concepts of God stand against the tests of the Scriptures and of life? Have we built enough mystery into our faith so that we are unshaken by a God who

- tells the Israelites to draw close to Him at the mount and then terrifies them? (Exodus 20:18-19)
- heals Naaman's leprosy but inflicts it on Elisha's servant? (2 Kings 5)
- promises to answer prayer (John 14:14) yet sometimes is silent?

- promises to never leave us (Hebrews 13:5) yet sometimes it feels as if He were absent?
- bottom line – allows seemingly bad things to happen to good people?

Have you noticed how the god we erect in our hearts usually looks strangely like ourselves, following *our* logic, acting as *we* think best? Then, when we anticipate God will "zig," but instead He "zags," we are hurt, disillusioned, even offended. Such responses – and we've all had them – are evidence of a faulty view of God, a graven image.

"Let God be true and every man a liar" (Romans 3:4). Imagine how different life would be if we could be so deeply planted in biblical faith that all God allows – good or bad – were equally met in our hearts with worship and awe, especially when it is different from our expectation.

DAY 17

Part 2: No Graven Image – Crises of Faith

Read Jeremiah 1:4-10; John 6:60-69

Anyone walking in relationship with the invisible God has suffered when their inaccurate conceptions of God – called "graven images" by Elisabeth Elliot – are exposed. For many this constitutes a crisis of faith, of which it could be said that if it doesn't kill you, it will make you stronger. Sadly not everyone's faith survives.

EARLY FOLLOWERS

One time after Jesus taught a really hard lesson that some of his followers didn't understand, some turned away. John 6:66-68, "From this time many of his disciples turned back and no longer followed him." The Twelve were equally as baffled by Jesus' hard teaching as were those who turned away, but their faith held up. Jesus asked, "You do not want to leave, too, do you?"…Peter answered him, "Lord, to whom shall we go? You have the words of eternal life." True disciples survive the test, but usually not without scars.

JEREMIAH

Jeremiah's crisis of faith came when he realized that the task he thought God had given him turned out to be something quite different. He cried out, "You deceived me, Lord, and I was deceived; you overpowered me and prevailed" (Jeremiah 20:7). Certainly Jeremiah knew God wouldn't trick or overpower him, but sometimes what we know and what we feel can differ greatly. At times like these, survival requires a trust rooted not in what we feel, but in who God is and in His ability to hold us fast to Him.

MOSES

One of Moses' crises of faith came when God responded in a way Moses didn't expect. God told Moses He would use him to deliver Israel from Pharaoh's hand. With the hopes of Israel raised, Moses confronts Pharaoh exactly as God instructed. Imagine Moses' alarm when this encounter results in Pharaoh increasing Israel's hardship! The Israelites' hearts are now soured toward Moses, who cries out to God, "Why, LORD, why have you brought trouble on this people? Is this why you sent me?" (Exodus 5:22). Disillusionment… It hurts.

God is who He is, not who we imagine Him to be. He does as He wills, not always as we expect. While clashes between the God that is and the God of our imaginations often go without being resolved in reason, they will always be resolved in a stronger faith in the true God…as long as we don't let our faith die.

> *"Don't look at God through the filter of your circumstances; look at your circumstances through the filter of who God is."*
>
> *- Stuart Briscoe*

DAY 18

Part 3: No Graven Image – Obedience is The Highest Service

Read Psalm 46:10; 95:6-7; 115:3

Elisabeth Elliot eventually wrote an autobiography of her first year as a missionary. The book, called *These Strange Ashes* recounts some of the heartbreaking losses marking that year for both her and her future husband, Jim Elliot.

Elisabeth and Jim had surrendered their lives to missionary service, but at the end of that year they felt it was all a waste. Elisabeth spent her year learning an unwritten language, in which she hoped to one day translate the Bible. But every note and language card was lost! Then her language helper, the only person on earth fluent in both languages she needed, was brutally murdered! As for Jim, he spent the year felling trees and making boards for a building project, but every last board was carried away in a flood!

What a waste that year of their life seemed! Or had it been?

Elliot ends her book with an apocryphal story well known to the early church, indicating that they, too, struggled with "graven images," i.e. reconciling the God of their minds with the God of reality.

The story goes like this:

One day Jesus said to His disciples, "I'd like you to carry a stone for me." So the disciples each went to find a stone. Peter, being the practical sort, looked for a small stone – after all, Jesus hadn't specified size. With the stone in his pocket, Peter joined the others and off they went when Jesus said, "Follow me."

A few hours later they were hungry. Jesus waved His hand over them, and behold! Their stones became bread! Peter's little bit of lunch was consumed in a minute, and there he sat, waiting for the others to finish.

Lunch over, Jesus made the same request and off the disciples went in search of another rock. This time Peter got it! He returned to the group with a boulder-size rock just as Jesus said, "Follow me." All afternoon Peter struggled to carry the boulder, but looked forward to his payoff at dinner. The sun neared the horizon just as they reached the sea. There Jesus said, "Now, throw your stone into the sea."

Peter and the others looked at him dumbfounded. Jesus sighed and said, "Don't you remember what I asked you to do? For whom were you carrying the stone?"

For whom do we carry the stone?

DAY 19

Part 4: No Graven Image – Which Image Will We Embrace?

Read John 20:19-21

YESTERDAY, WE READ THE STORY OF ELISABETH AND HER FUTURE husband, Jim Elliot, and how they despaired that their first year of missionary service had been a complete waste. In the novel version of her story, *No Graven Image*, Elisabeth refers to her disillusionment at that time as evidence of a faulty view of God, a "graven image," and it stung!

Ten years later, in 1975, Elisabeth's actual autobiography was published. The title, *These Strange Ashes*, was lifted from a poem of the same name by Amy Carmichael, a missionary to India whose writings Elliot thoroughly mastered.

The first two lines of Carmichael's poem are:

But these strange ashes, Lord, this nothingness,
This baffling sense of loss?

Through her own experience with "baffling losses," Elisabeth arrives at some profound conclusions, among which are these two:

Conclusion 1

"Faith's most severe tests come not when we see nothing, but when we see a stunning array of evidence that seems to prove our faith vain."

We pray, "Lord, we could use a little help here." The heavens are like brass.

"Lord, won't you please …
…heal?" No healing comes.
…bring my spouse back to me?" Divorce papers arrive.

...restore my relationship?" The woundedness deepens
...give us a child?" Another month of No.

Conclusion 2

"It is in our acceptance of what is given that God gives Himself." This truth, fully embraced today, will bring richness and stability to our lives, especially during times of disillusionment. It is in our times of acceptance of what is given – in the disappointment when we realize we still do not know Him as we ought – that God gives us Himself.

The crucifixion represented for the disciples a time when God "zigged" when they expected Him to "zag." Disillusioned and hurting, they cloistered themselves behind bolted doors. Heads in hands, they must have wondered, "What was all that about? So much for Jesus restoring Israel!" They had been wrong and it was crushing.

Suddenly, "Jesus came and stood among them and said, 'Peace be with you.' ... The disciples were overjoyed!...Again Jesus said, 'Peace be with you!'" (John 20:19-21)

"It is in our acceptance of what is given that God gives Himself." Shouldn't this be enough?

DAY 20

Sometimes Knowing What the Reason Is Not Is Enough

Read Jeremiah 31:20

YESTERDAY WE CONSIDERED THE FIRST TWO LINES OF AMY CARMI-chael's poem, "These Strange Ashes"

> *But these strange ashes, Lord, this nothingness,*
> *This baffling sense of loss?*

The next six lines are an answer to this question:

> *Son, was the anguish of my stripping less*
> *Upon the torturing cross?*
> *Was I not brought into the dust of death,*
> *A worm and no man, I;*
> *Yea, turned to ashes by the vehement breath*
> *of fire, on Calvary?*

The full poem merits study, but we focus for now on the stunning truth of these six phrases. As it turns out, suffering is not limited to man; God also suffers.

GOD THE SON SUFFERS

Jesus' suffering was not limited to His atoning death on the cross. He also suffered in His incarnation, when He forever altered His nature by adding "100-percent-man" to His 100-percent-God nature. He wept at Lazarus' tomb and mourned because of Israel's unbelief. He prayed with "fervent cries and tears."

GOD THE FATHER SUFFERS

In the days of Noah, God the Father "grieved that He had made man...His heart was filled with pain." Later He would long for errant Israel: "Is not Ephraim my dear son?...My heart yearns for him..."

GOD THE HOLY SPIRIT SUFFERS

God's Spirit can be grieved by disobedience and hardness of heart. Isaiah wrote, "[Israel] rebelled and grieved [God's] Holy Spirit" (Isaiah 63:10), and then the New Testament version, "And do not grieve the Holy Spirit of God" (Ephesians 4:30).

The truth that God can be trusted in suffering because He is a participant in it is a main premise of Timothy Keller's book, *Walking with God through Pain and Suffering*. Keller identifies God's participation in suffering as the "counterweight and the complement to the teaching that God is sovereign and uses suffering as a part of his often inscrutable purposes" (p. 147). His conclusion is that, while we cannot fully understand why God allows suffering and evil, "at least *we know what the reason is not*. It *cannot be* that he does not love us. It cannot be that he does not care" (p 121, italics mine).

So while we walk here below, where reasons for suffering are often allusive, can it be enough for now to know what the reason is not, that it is not for a lack of our Father's love that we suffer?

DAY 21
Part 1: Survivor's Guide to Suffering – Wonder
Read Job 38

PREPAREDNESS IS WHAT IS DONE IN ADVANCE OF A CRISIS TO HELP ensure survival. A banner, hung at the front of the classroom where a preparedness course was being taught, aptly said, "At the moment of truth, you will not rise to the level of expectation, but will fall to the level of training."

There is another kind of "preparedness," something we can do in our walk with Christ that will ensure not just survival in times of deep suffering, but that we thrive, whether that suffering is the result of a natural disaster or a personal crisis.

The first key to surviving suffering is to cultivate and maintain a sense of wonder and awe. God knits this into us in the womb, but years of life have a way of pummeling this out of us. In his book, *Recapture the Wonder,* Ravi Zacharias notes, "The tragedy with growing up is not that we lose childishness in its simplicity, but that we lose childlikeness in its sublimity." There's just something about the years that beats out of us our ability to rise in transcendent awe and wonderment at the simplest of marvels – a flower's beauty, a puff of wind, or a splashing wave.

Job definitely had lost his sense of wonder. From where he sat next to the ash pile, all he could see was incongruence: a God who had brought upon him great calamity even though he had done nothing so evil as to merit such treatment. It made no sense!

If what Job wanted was answers, it seems God felt what he really needed was more questions – 64 of them to be exact! Questions like: Where were you when I created the world? ... Where does darkness reside? ... Does the rain have a father? Do you send the lightning bolts on their way? Do they report to you, 'Here we are' (Job 38:6, 19, 28, 35)?

Sixty-four questions later Job was thoroughly overwhelmed. In a spirit of deep awe and humility, he answers God,

> You asked, "Who is this that obscures my counsel without knowledge?" Surely I spoke of things I did not understand, things too wonderful for me to know (Job 42:3).

Job still had no answer, but after his "interview" with God, he was content to allow wonder to fill that space. And suddenly, that was enough.

DAY 22

Part 2: Survivor's Guide to Suffering – Worship

Read 2 Chronicles 20:21-22

PREPAREDNESS IS NOT ONLY FOR SURVIVING DISASTERS; IT'S ALSO FOR surviving sorrows that come with living on a fallen planet. One piece in our "suffering preparedness" arsenal is to cultivate a strong sense of wonder. A second is worship, the heart directing extravagant love and adoration to God.

In the depths of deepest suffering, worship rises, at times, only by the strength of sheer obedience steadied by a resolute will. Sometimes our will even grabs our emotions on its way by, and the outlook brightens, the heart is soothed by an unforeseen drop of hope miraculously finding its mark through the darkness.

That is the power of worship.

BATTALIONS OF MUSICIANS

Good King Jehoshaphat understood the power of worship. In fact, he considered worship so powerful that he placed singers at the head of his army when they went into battle. Imagine the jeers of the enemy when they saw Judah's army advancing toward them for battle being led by musicians! According to the record, "As [the musicians] began to sing and praise, the LORD set ambushes against the men of Ammon and Moab and Mount Seir who were invading Judah, and they were defeated" (2 Chronicles 20:22).

That is the power of worship.

TIPS TO WORSHIP IN HARD TIMES

Worship out loud with words. Somehow hearing ourselves say a truth out loud presses it more deeply into our hearts and psyches than when it just floats around like a haze in our minds. What's more, our adversary and his lackeys, who cannot read our minds, hate hearing our worship! It's like a poke in their eyes.

Worship in gratitude. There is power in the simple act of saying thank you – especially to our Heavenly Father. Perhaps God tells us to "in all things give thanks," not just because it's right, but also because there's healing in it, all the more so when we feel least inclined toward gratitude.

Worship with song. Science cannot fully understand the connection that exists between humans and music. Music touches the whole person, making us tap our foot and move in time (physically), moving us to happiness and tears (emotionally), and raising us up in worship and exaltation (spiritually). And all this is achieved often without conscious effort on our part.

Suffering is warfare because our adversary, the ultimate opportunist, strikes hardest when we're down. Following Jehoshaphat's battle plan, we can rise up and overcome through worship.

DAY 23
Part 3: Survivor's Guide to Suffering –
Staying Under His Wings*

Read Psalm 91

*"Each new morn new widows howl, new orphans cry,
new sorrows strike heaven on the face."*
– William Shakespeare

IT IS STRANGE TO THINK OF HEAVEN BEING "STRUCK ON THE FACE" BY earthly suffering. Was this phrase a product of Shakespeare's poetic genius or his knowledge of God? Either way, it is accurate. In today's terms, this "strike" of heaven's face could be described as a gut punch to our Heavenly Father's love for His children.

The world is a dangerous place where people are killed every day from disease, accidents, war, and terrorists' murderous plots. The question is how do we stay safe in such a place?

Jesus wants us to be safe. He mourned because Jerusalem refused His safe protection. "Jerusalem, Jerusalem…how often I have longed to gather your children together, as a hen gathers her chicks under her wings, and you were not willing" (Matthew 23:37).

Jesus uses the metaphor of a mother hen covering her chicks from harm. The fire, the rain, hail, and cold all strike her, while the chicks under her wings are spared. That is what happened on the cross, when Jesus died in our place.

But does this protection extend beyond spiritual protection to physical protection? After all, we are presently living in a physical world and connected to physical bodies. While we long to be in our heavenly bodies, the transition into that body – death – is not usually anticipated with excitement.

Psalm 91 is another "under his wings" passage. While spiritual protection is included, this passage describes divine protection in graphically physical terms – protection from dangers such as pestilence, terror, arrows, plagues. While easily misinterpreted – such as Satan's twisted use of this passage when he tempted Jesus (Matthew 4) – this psalm clearly sets forth God's strong protection of our physical lives. Whatever the danger, God is our place of safety (verse 2), His promises are armor around us (verse 4), and He deploys angels to protect us (verse 11).

God is no bystander in the world's suffering; He is a participant in it. Our God, who wears skin and knows His way around the physical world, gives us this promise: "I will be with them *in* trouble (verse 15, italics mine)."

Survival tip: Get under Jesus' wings and rest in active belief (i.e. trust). Don't refuse as the people of Jerusalem did.

Thoughts inspired by a Timothy Keller sermon, "Satanic Exposition," given at Truth for Life Pastor's Conference, May 15, 2015.

DAY 24

Splash Overs of Hell

Read Psalm 91:14-16

If the name Joni Erikson Tada is widely known throughout much of North America, it is not because of her abilities as an artist, musician, or speaker, but because of her disability. She has been a quadriplegic for all but the first 16 years of her life when she had a diving accident. Decades of living with her disability have discipled her into a woman of extraordinary wisdom and beauty, making her one of the foremost voices speaking into our culture concerning the role of pain and suffering in the human experience.

I recently heard a radio broadcast in which Joni shared a conversation she and her husband had one day as they drove home from a treatment center where she had just been treated for cancer. Here is the transcript of that portion of the broadcast:

"My husband Ken was driving me home one day down the 101 freeway after a visit to the chemo clinic. As we were driving we were discussing how suffering is like a little splash over of hell – a little spoonful of hell come early, getting us thinking about and appreciating all that the Savior did to rescue us from that ultimate hell. And we talked about how suffering is, yes, a splash over of hell. It's awful; it's difficult; it's terrible.

"And then as we pulled up in the driveway and he turned off the ignition, we sat there for a moment and talked about, 'Well, then what are the splash overs of heaven?' Are they those easy, breezy bright days where birds are singing and everything is rosy?' We paused a moment, then decided, 'No, a splash over of heaven is finding Jesus in your splash over of hell.

"There's nothing more sweet, nothing more poignant and tender than finding Jesus in the midst of your hellish circumstances because then and only then do we find him to be ecstasy beyond compare. We don't see that side of Him apart from the adversity, but when we discover the Savior in the midst of our suffering...that is sweet."*

* Interview, Greg Laurie and Joni Eareckson Tada, "Joni Shares a Lifetime of Wisdom, http://www.harvest.org/radio/listen/2016-04-25. html?autoplay=1 , [9:25-10:50]

DAY 25

Part 1: Prayer – When the Heavens Are Like Brass

Read Hebrews 5:7; Mark 14:35-36; 15:34

PRAYER IS THE MOST CRITICAL PIECE IN THE SURVIVAL GUIDE FOR suffering. But what of those times when the "heavens are like brass" and prayer seems to "bounce off the ceiling?" Those clichés accurately describe a common experience in prayer. At such times one wonders, "What's wrong with me…my prayer…my faith?" Maybe nothing.

Jesus was a model pray-er. While the disciples saw Jesus perform amazing miracles, it was His prayer life that most intrigued them. "Lord, teach us to pray," they asked, not "teach us to do miracles." So, did Jesus, the model pray-er, ever experience the "heavens like brass" phenomenon? Judge for yourself based on heaven's response to one of Jesus' prayers.

THE REQUEST

The Gospels record that Jesus prayed, "Abba, Father,…everything is possible for you. Take this cup from me. Yet not what I will, but what you will" (Mark 14:36).

THE OUTCOME

God did not grant Jesus' request for the cup to pass from Him. The following day He died a horrific death, becoming our sin so we could become His righteousness (2 Corinthians 5:21). But then the worst happened. God turned away from Jesus, who cried out in anguish of spirit, "My God, My God, why have you forsaken me?"

The cup did not pass from Jesus. His Father did turn away from Him. Could the heavens at any other day in history seem more "like brass" than they did for Jesus on that day?

THE PROBLEM

Was it that Jesus lacked fervency in prayer? Not at all. So fervent was He that the intensity was breaking down His body, His sweat dripping like blood.

HEAVEN'S RECORD

What looks one way on earth can look quite different from heaven. While the Gospels describe eyewitness accounts of Gethsemane and Golgotha, Hebrews 5:7 reveals the testimony from heaven. This is how that account goes: "During the days of Jesus' life on earth, he offered up prayers and petitions with fervent cries and tears to the one who could save him from death, and he was heard because of his reverent submission."

According to heaven, Jesus' cries were heard, His tears seen, His prayer, "Not my will but yours," answered.

Though the heavens seemed like brass that day, it turns out they were as soft as the morning mist, just as they are for all who pray in reverent submission.

DAY 26

Part 2: Prayer – Worship in Reverent Submission

Read Hebrews 5:7

HEBREWS 5:7 SAYS THAT JESUS' PRAYER DURING HIS GREATEST TIME of crisis was heard "because of His reverent submission." Reverent submission is critical, not just in prayer, but for our daily lives. Without it, faith in our always-good, all-powerful, all-knowing God is impossible. The opposite of reverent submission is the spirit seen in the pathetic story of author Charles Templeton.

In his earliest ministry, Templeton traveled and preached with Billy Graham. Of the two, Templeton was said to have the stronger gifts, but he also had something Billy Graham didn't: growing doubts. Lee Strobel's interview with Templeton for his book, *The Case for Faith*, provides insight into this man's fall into agnosticism. His fall can be traced back to Templeton's disagreement with how God was running the planet. Safe to say, Templeton definitely lacked reverent submission.

According to Templeton, his faith finally broke under the weight of a picture in a Life magazine article on a devastating drought in Africa. In the picture, an African woman holds her dead baby, her face looking in agony toward heaven. Templeton says, "I thought, 'Is it possible to believe that there is a loving or caring Creator when all this woman needed was rain?'" (*The Case for Faith* p. 14) Templeton cites other reasons it was impossible for him to believe in the God of the Bible, such as the Bible's teaching on hell and the existence of evil and disease.

Nearing the end of his life in 1999, Templeton published, *Farewell to God: My Reasons for Rejecting the Christian Faith*, in which he explains why he abandoned his faith. One of those reasons, which he describes in especially horrific detail, is Alzheimer's disease. As it turns out, he had recently been diagnosed with the disease, which would take his life two years after his book was published.

Templeton's arrogance is slightly reminiscent of what Job was starting to sound like, but with one important difference: Job was humble and quickly repented of "darkening" God's character, while Templeton dug in his heels in human reasoning.

Prideful arrogance, the opposite of reverent submission, describes Templeton's error, and explains why his story ended very differently from Job's, and for that matter, Billy Graham's. Is there any more poignant way to illustrate the importance of reverent submission than the divergent trajectories of the lives of Templeton and Graham?

DAY 27

Part 1: Watch Your Mouth! – Job

Read Matthew 15:18; Job 38:2; 40:8; Ecclesiastes 4:2

JOB MUST HAVE BEEN STRUCK DUMB BEFORE GOD, WHEN AT THE END of his ordeal, God calls him to task for the foolish words he exchanged with his three "comforters." God says to Job, "Who is this that obscures my plans with words without knowledge...Would you condemn me to justify yourself?"

Job didn't sin with his mouth when he lost his wealth, servants, or even his precious children. He was still above reproach when he lost his health. Even when his comforters first arrived, he was fine. It wasn't until he opened his mouth that he got into trouble with God.

At the core of the argument between Job and his friends is the claim that God is too holy to allow the righteous to suffer. If suffering is the result of sin, Job must have committed a big one.

Job argued rightly that his trials were not due to sin. In fact, though he didn't know it, it was exactly because of his righteousness – not sin – that he was targeted for trouble. But, as so often happens in arguments, each frenzied attempt to make a point can leave one leaning slightly farther from the truth. Before long, Job was sounding way better than he really was, and God was sounding unjust.

The wise adage says, "Too much talk leads to sin. Be sensible and keep your mouth shut" (Proverbs 10:19 NLT).

There was another dynamic that contributed to Job's incremental movement toward error. It has to do with the power of a word once it is spoken. Have you noticed the sudden power a thought takes on the moment it is spoken? So the more Job heard himself talk, the more he believed his increasingly extreme hyperbole.

Working in three languages through the years has given me deep experience in mispronouncing words. After being corrected, sometimes I've thought, "I know I've heard it pronounced the other way." Upon further reflection, I realize that I had heard it the other way; when I myself had said it! A harmless example, but it illustrates the power that a word takes on once it is spoken.

Once Job realized his error, one can imagine him cradling his head saying, "What was I thinking?"

The point is not that God cannot handle hearing our faithless thoughts; but that maybe we cannot. We must be careful with the spoken word.

DAY 28

Part 2: Watch Your Mouth! – Jeremiah & Jonah

Read Psalm 94:11; 73:2, 15-17

JEREMIAH HAS BEEN CALLED THE APOSTLE PAUL OF THE OLD TESTAMENT because he, like Paul, was called from day one to suffer. Jeremiah can also be coupled with another prophet, the prophet Jonah. But in this case it is not due to the similarities but to the dissimilarities. As different as they both are, they each illustrate an important point about prayer in suffering.

Apart from the facts that Jeremiah and Jonah were both prophets and almost contemporaries (Jonah 100 years before Jeremiah), the dissimilarities begin:

- Jeremiah obeyed God's call from day one while Jonah fled God's call on day one.
- Jeremiah loved his people and pled with them to listen to God while Jonah hated the Ninevites and was angry when they listened to God.
- Jeremiah was persecuted and mocked by his people while Jonah was listened to and his message was accepted by the Ninevites.

But these two very different prophets illustrate the same important truth about prayer in suffering: we can be forthright and honest with God.

Jeremiah accuses God, saying, "Alas, Sovereign LORD! How completely you have deceived this people and Jerusalem…" (Jeremiah 4:10) On another occasion He accuses God of deceiving and utterly overpowering him (Jeremiah 20:7)!

As for Jonah, his answer to God's call, though non-verbal, was abundantly clear: he just ran away! If his lack of a verbal response is an indication of Jonah's reticence to speak frankly with God, three days in the belly of the fish must have cured him, because his prayers in the last chapter of Jonah actually sound a bit mouthy (Jonah 4)!

Returning once again to the story of Job, one must wonder why God accepted Jeremiah's and Jonah's frank, even mouthy objections, while calling Job to task for his?

Perhaps the difference is the audience. Jeremiah and Jonah both spoke to God while Job's words were spoken in public, to his comforters. "Who is this that obscures my plans...," God asks Job, "Would you discredit my justice? Would you condemn me to justify yourself?" (Job 38:2 and 40:8)

The issue is not that God cannot handle our "real" thoughts, it is more that other people may not be able to. The place to express questions, doubts, and accusations is before the One who already knows them, who already hears them in our consciousness. But double caution should be taken when expressing them to anyone else.

DAY 29
Our Happy God
Read Matthew 25:23

"Come and share your master's happiness"

THEOLOGIANS LIST 20 OR SO ATTRIBUTES OF GOD FROM SCRIPTURE. To finite man, these 20 attributes are like marbles in a jar, rarely touching and never mixing. But in reality, these attributes move and mix more like liquids. They are eternally co-existing, never conflicting, always moving and acting together in perfect harmony. This is our indescribable God.

One attribute emphasized in these daily thoughts is God's sovereignty – that disasters, death, or whatever the crises and the resulting suffering upon man may be, these are not cosmic "oops-es." Even through these acts God is achieving His good and loving purposes for all they touch. We've also considered God's love in suffering, that He is not aloof or a spectator, but rather a participant in it.

John Piper adds one more important characteristic about God: He is happy. Even in the midst of crisis and suffering, God is "blessed" (1 Timothy 1:11) or happy. This is possible because His happiness exists fully within Himself.

Even as God longs for the world to come to Him, that longing cannot diminish the happiness He has within Himself. He does not worry; the sea before His throne is as serene as glass, un-rippled by the winds of man's disobedience or the dark kingdom's assaults. His acts play out unthwarted; they, "…delight [his] heart because they reflect his glory…for in this his soul rejoices (John Piper, *Desiring God,* p. 53)."

Our God is happy! He fills the heavens with beautiful music (Revelation 14:1-3). Music so beautiful it would make Bach weep.

He is happy and loves celebration, filling the calendar of His people, Israel, not with fasts, but with feasts! He is happy, inviting us to join Him at a marriage supper to savor food without calories or cholesterol.

He is happy, enjoying walks with man in the cool of the day (Genesis 3:8).

This truth that ours is a Happy God, far from a thumb-in-the-eye to people stuck on a fallen planet, is a grand relief. As Piper has noted, who wants to spend eternity with an unhappy God? Knowing God is happy means we can be happy today in proportion to our intimate union with Him. We can be confident that the forever-afters of all who are found in Him will be happy.

DAY 30
The Parable of the Little Kite
Read John 16:33

THE LITTLE KITE WAS ECSTATIC. AFTER WEEKS OF BEING LOVINGLY assembled piece by piece, today his master finally would take him out to do what he was made to do: fly high! The sky was blue. The wind was stiff. The day was perfect!

In the field, the master runs with him and instantly the little kite takes to the wind. "Higher! Higher!" he squealed, and up he rose. "How beautiful it is up here!" he marveled.

But soon he realized he wasn't rising anymore. "It's this string! It's holding me back!" he realized, growing increasingly frustrated, then disgruntled, and then angry and sullen. "Why won't my master let me go? Why does he keep me tethered like this?" he brooded. Just then a strong gust of wind came and yanked him upward so hard it snapped the string. "Yea! I'm going higher. Higher. Higher!"

The end of the story of the little kite is not so glorious.

This is a metaphor for us as we walk through life. The wind will blow – which is fine because we're made for it. Indeed, we need the winds of trial and adversity to grow and purify our faith. But the string – our faith – must be tethered to our Heavenly Father. He will never let us go.

The question is, where is our faith anchored? Is it tethered to a graven image, a god of our own making? If so, when our wrong notions are discovered, and disillusionment settles in, will our string snap under the strain? Will we end up spiraling downward and crashing into a jumbled mess on the ground? Or will we look to the Lord to keep us airborne, holding us up when our own strength falters?

Crises and the suffering they cause will come. It's the stuff of a groaning planet, of people being made perfect day-by-day even as they are already perfect – "Already but not yet," as the saying goes.

Jesus' words to His grieving disciples the night before His crucifixion are a perfect conclusion to these thoughts: "I have told you these things, so that in me you may have peace. In this world you will have trouble. But take heart! I have overcome the world" (John 16:33).

PART 2
Discipled by Pain – One Man's Story

MANY WORDS COULD BE USED TO DESCRIBE WAYNE HANNAH: DEVOTed husband, loving father, pastor-shepherd, long-time staff member of Encompass World Partners* to name just a few. But before all that he was – and still is – a sufferer. But he's not just a sufferer; he's a model sufferer, who has earned the respect of those who know him best. We admire him because, 1) although he suffers almost every day with Crohn's Disease, it is rare that those around him know when he is having a rough day, and 2) he refuses to be defined by Crohn's.

In Part 2 we have the rare privilege of sitting at the feet of someone who has been discipled by pain. Many thanks to Wayne for graciously agreeing to write some thoughts about this gift God has entrusted to him: the gift of suffering.

* Formerly Grace Brethren Foreign Missions (GBFM), later Grace Brethren International Missions (GBIM)

The Nazareth Syndrome

THEY FOUND HIM IN THE SYNAGOGUE, OF COURSE.

Imagine what it must have been like. He grew up in this city. Nazareth: population of about 500. They all knew him and his mom and dad. Growing up, he must have been well known and popular. Though his father was a carpenter, he himself was highly educated, a rabbi. He certainly amazed the scholars down in Jerusalem that time when he was not yet a teen. It was no surprise that this native son had become a leader of multitudes, popular beyond imagination… and a doer of miracles.

The scene that unfolded that day in the synagogue in Nazareth is one of the most amazing in the life of Jesus. He is welcomed home, lauded, and praised by everyone. Everyone. Not only in Nazareth but also throughout the northern area of the country. His reputation as a leader, sage, and a teacher of the Scriptures was already legend; word of the miracles he had performed had spread throughout the land.

There in the synagogue the young Rabbi opened the scroll he had selected. It was a Messianic passage from Isaiah, describing the promised Messiah. After completing the reading, Jesus returned the scroll to the attendant and sat down. Opening his mouth he said, "Today this prophecy is fulfilled in your midst."

Every eye upon him, his next words, expounding on the meaning of the Messianic passage would shake them to their core. They were a certain pronouncement of his messiahship! There, in the midst of the people who had known him all his life, he positioned himself as the culminating center of the universe (as the Jewish people knew it), as the Savior and consummation of all their hopes, beliefs, dreams, and promises from Jehovah God!

At first they marveled, but quickly their joy flipped to a ferocious anger that fueled the mob to the point of wanting to murder Jesus. Were it not for his miraculous escape out of their midst, they would have thrust Jesus off the Precipice Mount to an early death.

Here's a paraphrase of what Jesus said that caused them to fly into a rage. (See Luke 4:14-27.)

"I am telling you that I am the Messiah, verified by the miracles I have done throughout Capernaum. You have heard about them. What you expect now is for me to do those same miracles right here in my hometown. But I must remind you that prophets have to say what is true, what fits with the plan of God even when it is not accepted or popular with people. This is especially true when the prophet has to tell the truth of God to the very people who are closest to him. So, you who have loved me most might like what I have to say the least."

At this pivotal moment, Jesus was seen as a threat to their desires, not as the Savior they expected. The crowd by their actions showed that they had decided they didn't like this kind of Messiah. "Let's kill this one and wait for a better one who will do what we deserve and expect. This can't be what Jehovah God had in mind for us!"

I WOULD HAVE BEEN FIRST IN THE MIRACLE LINE

What would you do if you had been there? If there had been a line forming of people who desperately needed a miracle, would you be in it? Me? I would have fiercely fought everyone to be first in the miracle line! I would not only have wanted a healing miracle, but like Jesus' Jewish community, I would have believed that I deserved one.

What would I have asked Jesus to do for me? I would have asked him to give me more guts. No, not courage, but actual intestines. There's a long story – more than 40 years long – explaining just why, but the short answer is wrapped up in two words: Crohn's Disease. My purpose here is not to talk about the personal pain and suffering that Crohn's has caused me, but to explain a few of the powerful lessons this suffering has taught me about God and the dramatic value of pain, suffering and crisis, in His loving plan for His children. What most people consider something to be rid of I have come to realize is something to embrace and even be thankful for.

MY STORY

The year was 1972. A recent college graduate, I headed to France for a two-year short-term missionary stint to work at the Chateau de St. Albain, a place of spiritual encounter and youth evangelism. Several months into my time there, I began to suffer quite regularly from harsh stomach pain. At first it was bearable, and I experimented with different dietary changes to see if that would help. After some weeks, the double-you-over pain became more intense and debilitating. Every seven or eight days the pain was accompanied by bouts of vomiting and high fever. I recall many occasions when my dear friends and co-workers and I would pray and cry out to God for relief and healing. I was always a small guy, weighing only about 125 pounds in those days. But, now I was slowly losing weight…120…115…110 pounds. Finally, Tom Julien, the France leader, and the staff gathered together to anoint me with oil and pray for God's healing. I intensely believed that God would heal me.

He didn't.

The next obvious step was hospitalization, and the doctors confirmed a diagnosis of ileitis, now called Crohn's Disease. There had been only a few recorded incidences of the disease in France, and they did not know what to do other than to recommend a diet of soft and bland foods. Sensing so strongly that my healing miracle was going to happen soon, I resisted the worsening pain and agonizing symptoms. It wasn't long before we all realized that the only option left was for me to return to the USA for treatment.

Within the hour after arriving home at the Dayton, Ohio, airport, our family doctor was examining me. The next day I was admitted at Ohio State University Medical Center in Columbus. My doctor there was a specialist, the head of the entire gastroenterology department, and the director of the first government-funded study of Crohn's Disease. I still prayed and begged God to be healed, of course. It was a huge encouragement to my soul, nonetheless, that God was showing his power, presence, and love to me through these events.

All options were pursued to avoid surgery; some things seemed to hold promise and some made me even sicker. It wasn't long before my condition became critical, and I weighed about 95 pounds. Without surgery, death was likely. On July 13, 1973, during a four-hour surgery, a portion of my small intestine was removed. The average adult has about 24 feet of small bowel, and as much as a fourth to a third was removed.

That's how it all began. I was twenty-four years old and full of optimism. So, I was imagining that after recovering from this surgery everything would be great with no more problems and no more disease. That optimism was seasoned with a bit of ignorance. Even the expert gastroenterologists weren't sure how to treat it. Sure, the doctors told me that there was no cure, but I believed that this was just a limit for the doctors. I had God on my side. This thing was a cinch for God to cure and I was confident that God not only could heal me, but that He had. He lined up the circumstances for me to find the best doctors and the best care, and the diseased areas had been cut out. God even arranged things so that the US government paid for all of my medical bills! So, I was sure that God had healed me.

But…He hadn't.

Over four decades have passed at the time of this writing and I still have Crohn's disease. In fact, I wrote part of this article during my regular three-hour IV drug infusion near my home in Atlanta, Georgia. While there have been some protracted periods when the disease was in remission, it has taken its toll. It has been the source of agonizing physical suffering. I have had seven intestinal resections to date. The shortened intestine has caused other problems, such as kidney stones--more than 30 passed or removed. When the intestine is damaged or restricted, the body forms other passageways called fistulas. Six of my more recent surgeries have been due to fistula abscesses and repairs. Accompanying the physical, of course, have been periodic bouts with discouragement, doubt, embarrassment, and occasional anger. Frustration has sometimes come from the misunderstanding by others of the disease. Oh, the number of bizarre and insulting cures and causes that have been suggested to me over the years!

My last resection in September of 2012 was certainly the toughest and most dramatic. At that point, the doctors at the Cleveland Clinic were convinced that my small intestine could no longer absorb enough nutrients to support life just by eating and drinking. Their attempts, however, at inserting a feeding tube into my vena cava vein resulted in major blood clotting. After several days in intensive care, Gina and I begged the doctors to release me and to let me at least try to eat and drink enough to stay alive. So, with the hope that I could take in and retain just enough nutrients and fluids to stay alive and praying to God, I was released. As I write this, it has been three-and-a-half years.

My diet became quite simple; I call it my "bring it on diet." Whatever food there is, bring it on! With lots of meals, three liters of fluids daily, hyper-intake of vitamins and mineral supplements, a couple of strategic medicines, and my abbreviated intestine has adapted and is working overtime to keep me alive.

So, now am I healed? Nope, still not.

As the reader can imagine, this disease has taken a great toll on my body. Low energy levels, pain and other limitations present lots of challenges to living a somewhat normal life. God has enabled me to continue working strongly in the ministry through the last 40 years. I pastored in two churches for nearly 20 years and have been serving in international missions for 20 more. Many Crohn's sufferers tend to give up on trying to lead a normal life. Many would never even think about traveling much if at all. Over the years in my extensive traveling, I have slept on floors, cots, and missionary kids' beds--in huts, cabins, hovels, the worst of hotels, in taxis, in dilapidated trucks and decrepit busses. I have eaten the most curious things from termites, grasshoppers, grub worms, horse meat, congealed pork blood, and mare's milk.

Even though I have traveled nearly two million miles and been in 45 countries, it has been amazing how I have been preserved from serious bouts with my Crohn's and related problems. Sure, there have been plenty of times when I have had to combat fatigue, pain, and other things that are just too gross to mention. But God has continued to enable and empower me to carry on and to preserve me through serious crises. This has been an extremely gratifying part of my walk with God, watching Him protect and strengthen me as I fulfilled my commitment to His call to full-time ministry. I thoroughly loved those many years in American church pastorates, but when the Lord called us back into an international ministry with Encompass World Partners, it was deeply meaningful. To have the extensive missionary involvement that we have had over these many years and yet, to be able to remain living in the United States near the health care I have needed, is a stunning example of God's grace and blessing.

LET'S GO BACK TO NAZARETH

So if I had been there that day in Nazareth would I have pushed my way to the front of that line for Jesus to heal me? Absolutely, if all I knew about Jesus was what those in Nazareth understood. But the Jesus I now know changes my response. The answer for most people would be obvious. I have to admit that it would be nice to be healed— no more chronic pain, no more swelling and bloating, no more bleeding, diarrhea, or surgeries. Who wouldn't want relief from all that?

If I had a choice to be healed of my disease and all of its attending issues today, would I choose healing? I have been asked this question several times. It may sound like a simple question with an easy answer. It's not. There would be reasons to say "no." There would be reasons to say "yes." I don't know. It's a good question that is loaded with implications. Of course, Jesus has never asked me if I wanted to be healed. I assumed for a long time that He did want that for me and there have been lots of people who believe that it is a foregone conclusion—that Jesus wants me and everyone else to be healed, too. The most misguided and hurtful are those who make the amount or strength of one's faith the prime factor in healing.

If Jesus' overriding desire was that everyone be healed, then how could He have indicted the people of His hometown and walked away from them having done no miracles? Does God want people healed? In the overwhelming majority of cases (probably somewhere above 99 percent) the answer is obviously something other than "yes." The answer, however, is not so much "no" as it is, "Keep asking until your request changes. But, you will discover in the process something you will appreciate more than if I healed you."

WHAT WE CAN LEARN FROM PAIN, SUFFERING, TRIALS, AND CRISES

1. The Planet and People Are Broken

People were broken in the garden and have not yet been fixed. Every human who has ever been born has been born broken. I am speaking, of course, in physical terms. No miracle has fixed that aspect of the fall. Death still is the inevitable end of our physical existence. Though the Bible doesn't say so, it's likely that everyone who was ever healed by God still eventually died. A multitude of people who feasted on bread and fish still had to eat again a few hours later. God picked particular situations to perform particular miracles for particular purposes. But the basic brokenness was never healed. If God healed me of my Crohn's, I still would wear glasses, occasionally get the flu, and have arthritis in my right leg.

The earth is broken and groans, and the result includes natural disasters: disasters that naturally happen. To some people the source of a crisis or catastrophe seems so important. Are crises a result of the natural processes of a broken planet? Yes. They nearly always are. Can God cause crises and suffering? Of course, but it's rare. Can Satan? Sure. Can people? Yep. The source isn't that important because most often we simply do not know. The reason for catastrophe or disease can be very important, but often we still do not know the reason even if we know the source. It is the response that is of supreme importance.

So, what's the source of my disease? Actually, no one knows. Did God give it to me? No. Allowing something is not the same as giving something. But did God intend for me to have it? Absolutely. After all, there are many cases of God's allowing and using disease, pain, suffering, and disasters to fit His purposes. Did Satan give it to me? I don't know. If so, then, consistent with the Scriptures, it would once again be only as God allowed it. Or, is it just the outcome of the physical decline in the human race and a manifestation of the deterioration of the human immune system? That is my firm belief. The source or the reason is not so important, and I no longer even wonder or care. How I respond to my illness, however, is what is most important.

2. The Believer's Response to Crisis, Suffering, and Pain

The Bible is consistent in its instruction about how to respond to crisis and suffering. Job's tragedies were all a result of Satan's taunting of God. It was Job's exemplary testimony of faith that provoked it. He got hammered because he was so righteous. It was Job's profound faith that also enabled him to withstand the assaults of the wicked one. Throughout the New Testament the writers remind us that suffering is to be welcomed, not resisted, met with rejoicing, and recognized as a source of learning and the deepening of our faith.

"Dear brothers and sisters, when troubles of any kind come your way, consider it an opportunity for great joy" (James 1:2). Really! James' words might be easy to swallow if one is talking about having a head cold or a broken leg. But these words equally apply to the perspective that one should have toward any "troubles" no matter their intensity or severity. James goes on to explain why, the reason. When faith is put to the test, it grows your endurance. When endurance grows fully, you will be perfect and complete, needing nothing. The rejoicing attitude we are to have is not in expectation of a healing or a life without crisis. It is a rejoicing that points to the greater goal that our faith in Christ produces—needing nothing.

3. God's Plan For Us Requires Suffering

God's Plan for us is so different from the one we have for ourselves. I love that passage in Hebrews 12 that reminds us that earthly fathers do not know how to discipline their children like God does. It's so true. The proper balance between correction and encouragement is seldom achieved. Unbalanced correction can so easily become abuse. Unbalanced encouragement can so easily become indulgence. The default impulse in the heart of most parents is protectionism. Since parents do not have the sovereign and eternal perspective of God, they are much more protective than even He is. Consequently one parenting skill that is largely missing from an earthly father's skills in disciplining his children is the use of pain. "No discipline is enjoyable while it is happening; it's painful (v. 11)." Believe me, if my parents could have stopped me from being afflicted by this disease, they would have. But God didn't, and He's the perfect Father, knowing what will make me a better person. Because of their love, my parents would more likely have insulated me from some of the greatest lessons of life that I could learn only through my suffering. Because of God's love for me, He dare not withhold the pain and suffering. As hard as it is to apply the same biblical principles to major catastrophes and suffering on a grand scale, they are nonetheless true and applicable.

4. God Himself Suffers

God completely understands our suffering because He suffers, too. Many of the negative emotions that are attributed to God – anger, wrath, agony, displeasure, grieving, etc. – are expressions of suffering. When His will and love are not obeyed, He experiences pain.

Something changed in the Godhead when Jesus took on human form. God no longer saw and felt the human experience from a single, outside perspective as almighty God. When God became as much human as divine, He did so permanently. Today Jesus is still in human form (Philippians 3:20-21; Acts 1:9-11). We believers relish the image of Christ in His glorified state, sitting in authority and power at the right hand of the Father.

To see Jesus as a suffering Savior is a less than satisfying image to most of us. We imagine that once Jesus bowed His head and gave up His spirit that His suffering was finally over. When we gaze deeply into His suffering – the persecution, beatings, shameful debasement, the unfathomable agony of soul that squeezed blood into His sweat, the fool's crown, the thrust spear – we feel pain, anger, sympathy, and sadness. Because we know the whole story, we can only imagine His pain as we view it backwards through our fuller knowledge of His regained life and power. But Philippians reminds us that we cannot know the Savior completely without comprehending and experiencing the fellowship of His suffering.

God is still suffering, not on the cross but because of the cross. He longs for the completion of the redemption when all things are finally made new. It is difficult to conceive of a God of love with suffering, loss, and pain. The offer of His love and subsequent sacrifice is received or rejected. The accepted sacrifice brings joy to Christ. Rejected, it brings agony.

We have not well understood or have forgotten that at the instant that death crashed into human existence through sin, God began sharing in the effects of this death in His own person, an inexplicable pain of betrayal and separation within His once holy creation. He is touched and affected by the suffering of His children. Contrary to the skeptic's view of God, He is anything but an aloof, passive, or self-interested God. Just as in the cross of Christ, perhaps His greatest purposes still come from the greatest suffering.

5. God's Power Works Best in Weakness

One of the passages of Scripture that has been a great encouragement to my soul in the face of my weakness is 2 Corinthians 4, which tells us that our bodies are made of clay yet we have the treasure of the Good News in them. This shows that the superior power of this treasure belongs to God and doesn't come from us. And a few chapters later Paul speaks of the gift he was given, a messenger of Satan to torment him and keep him from being proud. "Three different times I begged the Lord to take it away. Each time He said, 'My grace is all you need. My power works best in weakness.' So now I am glad to boast about my weaknesses, so that the power of Christ can work through me. That's why I take pleasure in my weaknesses, and in the insults, hardships, persecutions and troubles that I suffer for Christ. For when I am weak then I am strong (12:9-10). When I am strong, I am strong. When I am weak, He is strong. God's strength and my strength combat against each other and cannot occupy the same space at the same time.

6. Suffering and Crisis Are Not All about Those Who Suffer

Would you rather be healed or the healer? Would you rather be the hurting or the comforter? Would you rather be starving or the one who feeds the hungry? Would you rather be in the earthquake or the relief worker? Would you rather be me, or Gina, my wife? I suspect that none of us wants to be the one who suffers. The task of the healer, however, is not an easy one either. When I reflect on the years of sacrificial love and care that Gina has graciously provided me, I am immensely grateful. From the descriptions of my suffering one can just imagine how many anxious hours she has spent sitting in surgical waiting rooms, in hospital rooms, doctors offices, ICU departments, and in those back bedrooms of our home feeling worn down by sleepless nights and sometimes, fear. The very love she has for me is the biggest drain to her energy. The depth of her caring is often the measure of her fatigue.

Crises, suffering, sickness, and brokenness provide an avenue for the expression of God's love through others. My illness isn't just for me. It is also for Gina. God gave her very distinct gifts that exactly match my need. She is one of the most practical, efficient, and administratively wired people I know. It's the way she serves. It's the way she shows love. Her attention to detail and tactics surrounds me with a sense of security and confidence. It contrasts with my bent toward feelings, analysis, emotion, and the relational side of things. She was given those abilities for my benefit, of course, but also for hers. In the expressing of who she is there is a fulfillment of God's design and a satisfaction in being a conduit of the love of God to the hurting. My crisis is her opportunity.

In the same way, I believe that since the world is broken and catastrophes happen, God gifts and mobilizes people to be responders to these tragedies—to be ministers of love, mercy, and healing to the broken, the diseased, the outcast, the abused, and to the loved ones of those who perish. Crises are not caused for the love of God to shine out, but since they are inevitable, so is the grace and love of God to distribute His ambassadors of mercy throughout the world to respond to the pain. The tragedy is not only about the one who suffers.

THERE IS ALWAYS AN EPILOGUE

As this story has indicated in numerous places, there is more to come. There is a meta-story and an aftermath that in the moment cannot be seen. Some catastrophes happen in a moment, some throughout a lifetime or an age. Throughout the Scriptures we witness many disasters and crises. Every one of them had a greater good that was part of the story. We know this because we have the Scriptures, of course. Then why can't we recognize that today God has a greater good in mind as He allows the brokenness of His creation to crumble and run its course.

Six days after the 2004 Tsunami in southern Thailand, I was riding and walking through the rubble of this devastated coastline of Khao Lak. The pictures in my mind still bring an ache to my soul—the stench of the morgues and the smell of the smoke from the Buddhist crematoriums, the now non-existent towns, the huge fishing boats that were deposited on high inland hills, the wailing of the Thai and tourist families as they recognize the picture of their loved one(s) posted on the walls of the dead, a child's flip-flop wedged into the branches of a ravaged tree.

Along with lots of other people, I returned to the scene as a responder to this crisis, bringing teams and aid. The years have passed and I have had the opportunity to talk with friends and other workers who continued to minister in this coastline area of Thailand. What a contrast and a joy to hear of the many Thai who have become followers of Jesus Christ and of the existence now of many new church communities in that area. While God's epilogue doesn't necessarily reduce the ache of the tragic scenes embedded in my mind and heart, His epilogue does remind us that God has a plan and a purpose for suffering that is higher and greater.

Nazareth response…or the response of faith?

So which will it be? Get a Savior that works like we want Him to work and does what we want Him to do? Or will we choose to be okay with what God wants to do, when He wants to do it, and in the way He wants to do it?